SECRETS OF THE DINOSAU

T0178979

PLATES

TAIL SPIKES

USE SCANNER
TO CLEAR
INTERFERENCE

AUTUMN PUBLISHING

AUTUMN
PUBLISHING

Illustrated by Jake Hill
Written by Ashwin Khurana

Designed by Richard Sykes and Jamie Abraham
Edited by Katie Taylor

Published in 2023
First published in the UK by Autumn Publishing
An imprint of Igloo Books Ltd
Cottage Farm, NN6 0BJ, UK
Owned by Bonnier Books
Sveavägen 56, Stockholm, Sweden

Manufactured in China. 0723 001
10 9 8 7 6 5 4 3 2 1

Library of Congress Cataloging-in-Publication
Data is available upon request.

ISBN 978-1-83771-667-8
autumnpublishing.co.uk
bonnierbooks.co.uk

CONTENTS

WHAT ARE DINOSAURS?

Dinosaurs roamed the Earth for more than 170 million years. Although the word dinosaur means "terrible lizard" in Greek, they were not actually lizards but a separate family of reptiles, like snakes. Based on the shape of their hips, there are two main dinosaur types: Saurischian (lizard-hipped) and Ornithischian (bird-hipped).

Many prehistoric plants still grow today, from Wollemi pines and soft tree ferns, to beautiful flowering plants like magnolias and allspice.

Carnivores (meat-eaters) had sharp, pointy teeth to rip into prey, while herbivores (plant-eaters) used their rake-like teeth to strip leaves from tree branches.

The smallest dinosaurs were no bigger than today's domestic cat or bird, but the average dinosaur was roughly the size of a car.

THE WORLD OF THE DINOSAURS

Dinosaurs lived between 245 and 66 million years ago (MYA). The Mesozoic Era, which includes the "Age of the Dinosaurs," can be further split into three distinct periods: Triassic, Jurassic, and Cretaceous. During this time landmasses broke up, which led to different dinosaurs evolving separately across the planet.

PREHISTORIC / TODAY

TRIASSIC PERIOD 252-201 MYA

The first dinosaurs roamed a supercontinent called Pangea. There were forests and oases, but the Triassic landscape was generally dry. Triassic dinosaurs included the four-ton herbivore Plateosaurus, and the cat-sized carnivore Marasuchus.

Sauropods were the tallest dinosaurs, reaching up to 60 ft—this is equal to a six-story building!

Flying reptiles called pterosaurs may have had brightly colored feathers. Carnivorous dinosaurs, known as theropods, also had feathers to keep them warm.

All dinosaurs laid eggs. The earliest eggs had soft shells but, as dinosaurs evolved, their eggs became hard, offering extra protection for the embryo growing inside.

Unlike the angled legs of other reptiles like crocodiles or lizards, the legs of dinosaurs were straight and upright.

JURASSIC PERIOD 201-145 MYA

Pangea separated into two regions, Laurasia and Gondwana. More rainforests and floodlands started to appear. The scaly Scelidosaurus and predator Kileskus, the oldest member of the tyrannosaur family, lived at this time.

CRETACEOUS PERIOD 145-66 MYA

Earth's continents continued to shift, providing the perfect conditions in some regions for flowering plants and lush forests. New dinosaurs appeared, including the 66-ton Argentinosaurus, the horned Triceratops, and the fearsome T. rex.

KING CARNIVORE

Living at the end of the Cretaceous Period in present-day USA, the imposing T. rex used its incredibly powerful jaws, sharp teeth, and outsized brain to outsmart and tear apart anything in its way.

BONES / SKIN

This huge hunter had a very keen sense of smell and exceptional eyesight, perfect for scoping out prey in the distance.

Once the front teeth gripped the prey, the sharp side teeth sliced through its flesh. The tough back teeth could crush bones.

THEROPOD HUNTERS

The most diverse group of lizard-hipped dinosaurs are known as theropods. From the chicken-sized Microraptor to the terrifying T. rex, all theropods were carnivores, walked on two hind legs, and used their forelimbs and hands to grasp and tear apart flesh.

PACK HUNTERS

Most paleontologists (dinosaur experts) agree that small theropods hunted in packs, like lions or wolves today. This cooperative behavior allowed them to stick together and take down prey larger than themselves. Some scientists believe that larger theropods may have also worked in this way.

By wagging its sturdy tail, T. rex stopped itself from falling over, and maintained fantastic balance while chasing its prey.

This predator would eat anything that moved—even its own kind—by pulverizing the prey's flesh, then swallowing chunks of it before digestion.

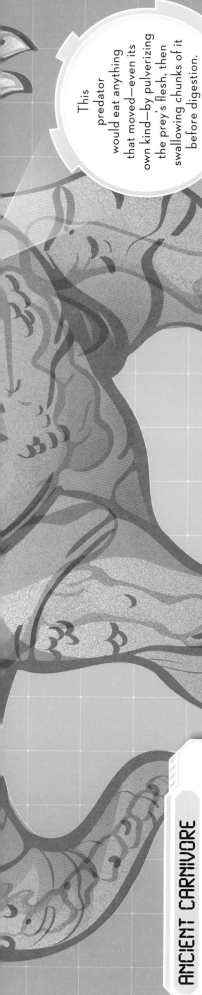

ANCIENT CARNIVORE

Before theropods, ferocious reptiles such as Postosuchus—a close cousin of crocodiles—roamed the landscape in present-day North America.

SPINOSAURUS AMBUSH

Bigger than the mighty T. rex, the sail-backed Spinosaurus is the only known dinosaur to have lived both on land and in the water. In the murky riverbanks of present-day Africa, this Cretaceous theropod quietly stalked fish before using its crocodilian teeth to grasp and eat its prey.

Each T. rex foot stomp remained constant—perfect for the surprise attack, as the prey could not tell if the beast was near or far.

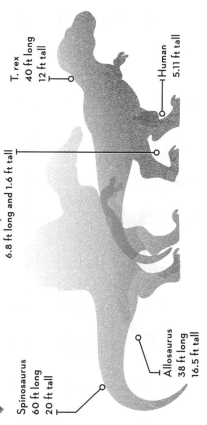

T. rex
40 ft long
12 ft tall

Human
5.11 ft tall

Velociraptor
6.8 ft long and 1.6 ft tall

Allosaurus
38 ft long
16.5 ft tall

Spinosaurus
60 ft long
20 ft tall

BIG, BIGGER, BIGGEST

Humans would have been dwarfed by many prehistoric predators. The ferocious Allosaurus roamed 145 million years ago, but 76 million years later T. rex dominated the landscape. Spinosaurus—the biggest ever theropod—evolved 99 million years ago, then 20 million years later came the small but vicious Velociraptor.

DINOSAUR DEFENSES

The world of the dinosaurs famously included some of the most powerful predators ever known, such as T. rex and Allosaurus. Plant-eating animals that lived alongside them had to develop equally powerful tools to defend themselves.

The bones inside the tail of a Euoplocephalus formed a heavy club that could inflict stunning blows on attackers.

ARMOR PLATING

Ankylosaurs were a group of dinosaurs with armor plating all over their bodies, making them a formidable foe for any predator. Even their eyelids had armored scales! Some species, such as Euoplocephalus and Ankylosaurus, were also equipped with bony clubs in their tails that they could use to batter attackers.

SPIKY STEGOSAURS

Stegosaurus fossils have been found with spines up to 35 in long. That's as long as an adult human's entire leg!

Some Allosaurus fossils have holes punched through the leg bones. Scientists believe this may be evidence of fearsome blows from a Stegosaur's spikes.

Stegosaurus and its relatives had long spikes at the ends of their tails, which they could lash against the bodies of predators.

HORNS AND FRILLS

Triceratops belonged to a group of dinosaurs called Ceratopsians. Many animals in this group had horns on their heads and snouts, which they used to fight back against attackers. The frill of bone behind their heads shielded their necks from biting attacks.

The neck frills of most Ceratopsians were supported by a heavy frame of bone, making them strong enough to resist the powerful jaws of giant predators.

TOUGH NUTS

SKULL / BRAIN

The thick skull of a Pachycephalosaurus protected a brain that was only about the size of a walnut.

Pachycephalosaurus and its relatives had a plate of bone up to 8 in thick in the tops of their skulls. They might have used their powerful headbutts to settle arguments within a herd, as well as to drive away predators.

TRUE GIANTS

The biggest dinosaurs are known as sauropods. From Brachiosaurus to Diplodocus, they are all identified by their massive bodies and relatively small heads, along with their bendy necks and long tails. Roaming the planet for around 140 million years, these lizard-hipped giants only ate plants.

APATOSAURUS

Growing up to 76 ft long, the late-Jurassic giant Apatosaurus lived in present-day USA. It is also sometimes called Brontosaurus.

Rather than grinding plant material, this giant swallowed it whole. Stomach stones called gastroliths helped to break down and digest the food.

Like an elephant, Apatosaurus had cushioned pads on the bottom of their feet for support. Their footprints would be up to 3 ft wide.

BIG, BIGGER, BIGGEST

Today, the giraffe and African elephant tower over all other animal species. However, they would have been dwarfed by some of giants that once roamed Earth. Even one of the smallest sauropods, Saltasaurus (a late Cretaceous creature that lived in present-day Argentina) would eclipse anything that exists today.

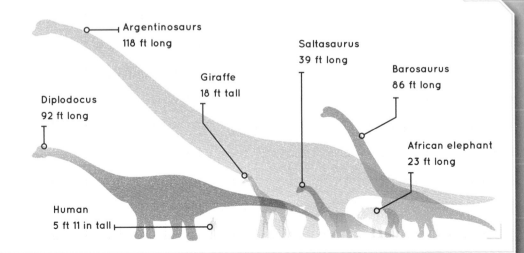

Argentinosaurs
118 ft long

Saltasaurus
39 ft long

Giraffe
18 ft tall

Barosaurus
86 ft long

Diplodocus
92 ft long

African elephant
23 ft long

Human
5 ft 11 in tall

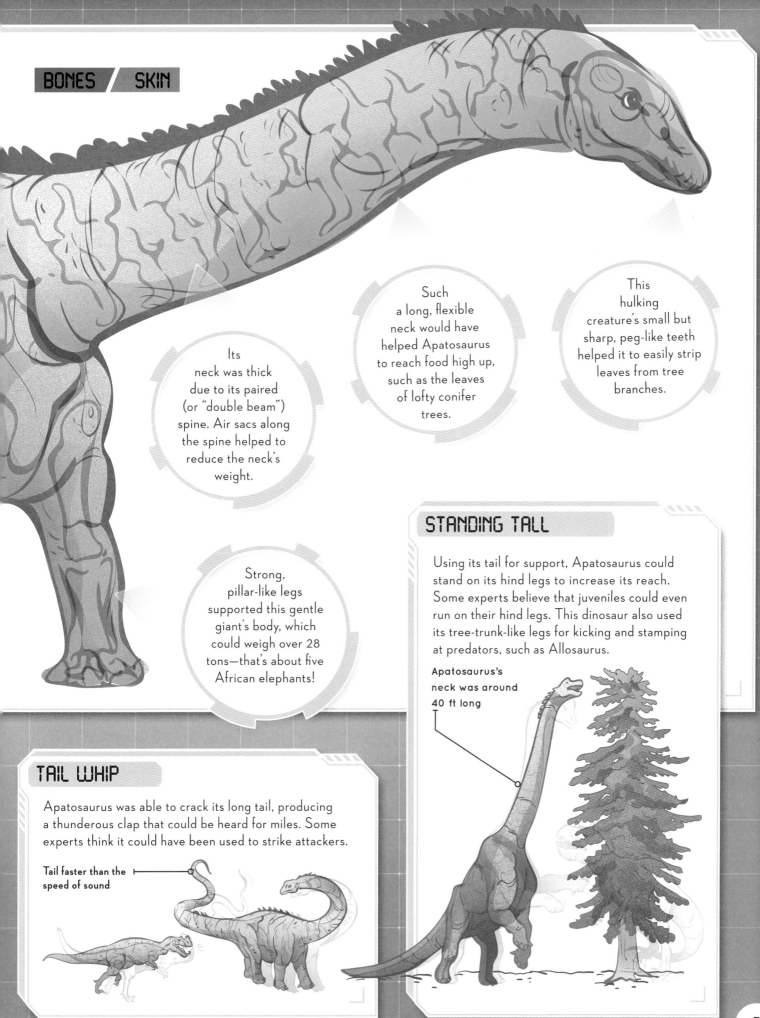

BONES / SKIN

Its neck was thick due to its paired (or "double beam") spine. Air sacs along the spine helped to reduce the neck's weight.

Such a long, flexible neck would have helped Apatosaurus to reach food high up, such as the leaves of lofty conifer trees.

This hulking creature's small but sharp, peg-like teeth helped it to easily strip leaves from tree branches.

Strong, pillar-like legs supported this gentle giant's body, which could weigh over 28 tons—that's about five African elephants!

STANDING TALL

Using its tail for support, Apatosaurus could stand on its hind legs to increase its reach. Some experts believe that juveniles could even run on their hind legs. This dinosaur also used its tree-trunk-like legs for kicking and stamping at predators, such as Allosaurus.

Apatosaurus's neck was around 40 ft long

TAIL WHIP

Apatosaurus was able to crack its long tail, producing a thunderous clap that could be heard for miles. Some experts think it could have been used to strike attackers.

Tail faster than the speed of sound

FLYING REPTILES

Long before birds or bats, pterosaurs ruled the skies. These flying reptiles thrived alongside the dinosaurs for 150 million years. Some were no bigger than a small bird, while others had a wingspan reaching 39 ft, which is about the same length as a whale shark!

SKY KING

About 90 to 100 million years ago, a short-tailed, long-legged reptile known as Pteranodon could be seen flying over present-day USA, Asia, Europe, and South America. They lived in huge flocks, soaring over oceans while looking for fish to pick off.

20 ft wingspan

Three small-clawed fingers at the bend of each wing were too small for gripping food, so they probably helped Pteranodon with walking.

TINY PREDATORS

Today's bats are similar to the small pterosaur Anurognathus, with lightweight wings, sharp teeth for chewing insects, and furry bodies. This pterosaur, however, had large eyes adapted for seeing clearly at night, while bats navigate at night using sound waves that bounce off objects, known as echolocation.

Lightweight wings

20 in wingspan

Furry bodies

This creature had a furry body, like most pterosaurs. This would have been important to keep them warm and regulate body temperature.

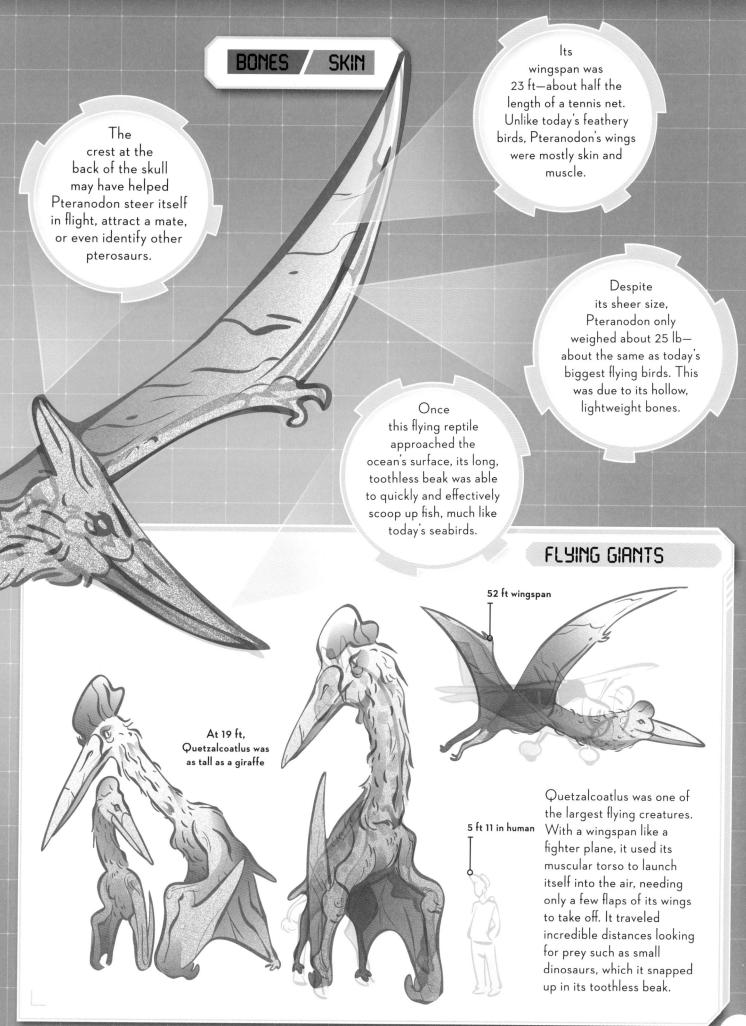

BONES / SKIN

The crest at the back of the skull may have helped Pteranodon steer itself in flight, attract a mate, or even identify other pterosaurs.

Its wingspan was 23 ft—about half the length of a tennis net. Unlike today's feathery birds, Pteranodon's wings were mostly skin and muscle.

Despite its sheer size, Pteranodon only weighed about 25 lb—about the same as today's biggest flying birds. This was due to its hollow, lightweight bones.

Once this flying reptile approached the ocean's surface, its long, toothless beak was able to quickly and effectively scoop up fish, much like today's seabirds.

FLYING GIANTS

52 ft wingspan

At 19 ft, Quetzalcoatlus was as tall as a giraffe

5 ft 11 in human

Quetzalcoatlus was one of the largest flying creatures. With a wingspan like a fighter plane, it used its muscular torso to launch itself into the air, needing only a few flaps of its wings to take off. It traveled incredible distances looking for prey such as small dinosaurs, which it snapped up in its toothless beak.

SEA MONSTERS

Today, creatures like the Great White Shark and Blue Whale rule the oceans, but during the "Age of the Dinosaurs," the water was dominated by massive marine reptiles. Millions of years later, a terrifying, gigantic shark roamed the prehistoric seas.

BONES / SKIN

MOSASAUR

Between 75 and 69 million years ago, a group of marine reptiles called mosasaurs were the ocean's top predators. Reaching 50 ft in length, these excellent, web-footed swimmers ate everything and anything, even their own kind.

SCARY SCALE!

Use your lens to see how a scuba diver measures up to today's top ocean predator, the Great White Shark, which can grow up to 20 ft long.

WHAT DID THEY EAT?

Tiny trilobites, an extinct species related to spiders, were some of the earliest prey for many prehistoric sea animals. Molluscs including ammonites, which grew in an unusual knotted shape, were popular food sources, as were belemnites (that looked more like squid). Giant bivalves such as clams were popular with predators, as were many fish such as the coelacanth, which still exists today.

| AMMONITE | CLAM |

| COELACANTH | TRILOBITE |

MEGALODON

Between 17 and 3 million years ago, the ferocious Megalodon cruised the seas, munching on dolphins and whales. An adult was 60 ft long, which is three times longer than a great white shark.

ICHTHYOSAUR

Looking more like dolphins, ichthyosaurs lived during the entire timespan of the dinosaurs. They could grow to a whopping 85 ft in length, and used their 200 cone-shaped teeth to eat fish and squid.

PLIOSAUR

With their paddle-like limbs, 50-ft-long pliosaurs swam a bit like penguins. Living between 220 and 70 million years ago, this group of sea reptiles had sharp, knife-like teeth, perfect for ripping into their prey.

ARCHELON

From 80 to 66 million years ago, a giant sea turtle known as Archelon swam the oceans hunting jellyfish and crustaceans. They grew up to 13 ft long—more than twice the length of the biggest turtle today, the Leatherback.

DINO BABIES

Like most reptiles today, dinosaurs laid eggs. The largest eggs were laid by the largest dinosaurs—the sauropods. Some dinosaurs may have looked after their young for some time after hatching, while other babies were left to fend for themselves.

OVIRAPTOR

This parrot-like dinosaur laid two eggs at a time in a clutch of 30 or more. The mother would arrange the eggs in a circle and bury them until they hatched.

MAIASAURA

Maiasaura lined its nest with rotting vegetation to keep its eggs warm. Fossil evidence suggests that this large dinosaur looked after its offspring for up to several months after they hatched, since young Maiasaura were very vulnerable to hungry predators.

SAUROPODS

Experts have located nesting colonies where sauropods would have laid eggs to keep them warm, but it is unlikely the parents stuck around once they hatched.

T. REX

The most fearsome of all predators, T. rex used its large snout to carefully pick up fragile eggs and small offspring, keeping them protected and warm. Crocodiles do something similar today.

INSIDE EGGS

Like birds, dinosaur embryos would have fed on the yolk inside the egg. An egg, which could be up to 12 in long depending on the dinosaur, could take three to six months to hatch.

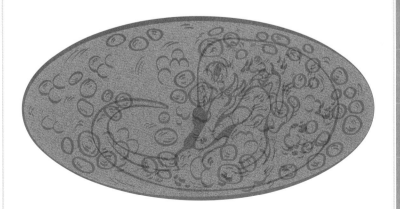

THE END OF THE DINOS

Dinosaurs, pterosaurs, and large marine reptiles could not survive the impact of a huge asteroid that crashed into Earth 66 million years ago. This mass extinction event wiped out about three quarters of all land animals and plant life.

THE ASTEROID

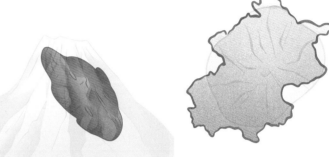

A massive asteroid slammed into Mexico's Yucatán Peninsula. The place where it landed is called the Chicxulub crater.

Slamming into Earth with the force of a million atomic bombs, this asteroid was around 6.2 miles wide—about the same size as the world's biggest mountain, Mount Everest.

EFFECT OF IMPACT

After impact, a huge plume of hot rocks was cast out into the sky before raining down on the animals below. Eventually, dust settled throughout the world and darkened the skies, blocking out sunlight and cooling the planet. Plants died and herbivores starved to death, which meant that carnivores had nothing to eat either.

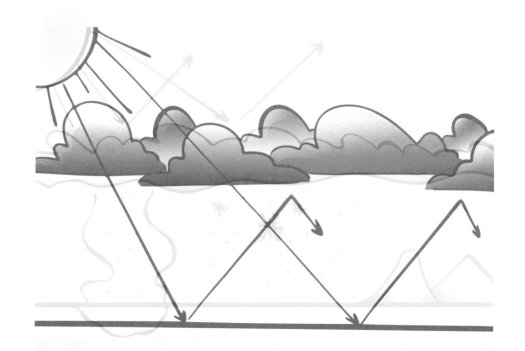

LAND AND SKIES

Dinosaurs and pterosaurs did not stand a chance against the falling debris, fires and earthquakes. But birds—which are direct descendants of small, bird-like theropods— flourished, possibly due to their small size and ability to fly. Many mammals also survived by hiding in burrows and using their fur to keep warm.

OCEANS

The asteroid caused the extinction of many ocean giants like ichthyosaurs, but overall, marine life—both in oceans and freshwater lakes—fared much better than land animals. Sharks, turtles, and crocodiles, along with marine mammals like whales and dolphins, were able to survive and evolve.

FOSSILS

In the right conditions (and with enough time), a living thing can turn into a fossil, which is the preserved, physical evidence of a plant or animal. Paleontologists rely on fossils to learn more about prehistoric times—after all, there were no cameras back then!

HOW FOSSILS FORM

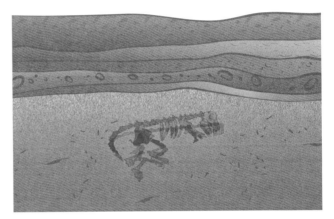

After a dinosaur dies, its flesh might be eaten by hungry animals and other dinosaurs. If not, its flesh naturally decomposes and the remaining skeleton sinks into a layer of mud, where it becomes buried.

More mud, sand, volcanic ash, and lava build up in thick layers on top of the skeleton. During this time, the skeleton becomes increasingly squished and flattened into the mud, often crushing some parts of it.

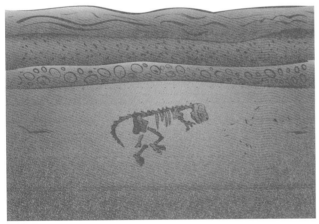

Over millions of years, these heavy layers turn into hard, sedimentary rock in a process known as lithification. While this happens, water seeps into the skeleton and leaves behind minerals that turn the bones into stone, creating a fossil.

The planet has changed dramatically since the dinosaurs, and in many places, the earth has moved upwards (this is called "uplift"). As wind, water, and ice slowly wear away the once-submerged rock, the fossilized skeleton hidden for millions of years can now be found.

TYPES OF FOSSIL

BODY FOSSILS

Body fossils are the mineralized outlines of bones, feathers, skin, egg shells, and parts of plants such as branches or stems. They can be small like a shark's tooth, or big like a dinosaur's skull. The are the most common type of fossil.

COPROLITES

Coprolites are prehistoric poo. They are trace fossils, which means they do not belong to the animal's body. Fossilized waste not only teaches us what an animal ate, but also helps to explain what other animals and plant life existed at the same time.

SEASHELLS

The process of decomposition (breaking apart) begins soon after a sea creature with a shell (like an ammonite) dies. As the animal's soft tissue decomposes, the hard shell becomes buried in the seabed, leaving much of it very well preserved.

PLANTS

When the materials that make up an ancient tree are replaced with minerals, such as calcium, the tree becomes petrified (turns to stone). Other plants, such as ferns, can also turn into fossils when dissolved minerals fill up the space inside their cells.

DINOS TODAY

The last mass extinction occurred 66 million years ago and killed most of the animals on Earth, but many birdlike dinosaurs survived. These theropods—which include the vicious Velociraptor—are in fact ancestors of modern birds, and share many features such as excellent vision and feathers.

Like their theropod ancestors, modern birds have incredible eyesight. An ostrich's huge eyes mean it can see a moving object up to 1.8 miles away.

DINOS DESCENDANTS

The way modern birds stand and walk is inherited from theropods, including how they stand upright on two legs, how they crouch, and their overall balance.

Modern birds have feathers for keeping warm, waterproofing, and display. Most birds also use feathers to fly, but ostriches cannot do this.

Most dinosaurs laid hard-shelled eggs, just like modern birds. Dinosaurs also made nests to protect their eggs and keep them warm, as birds do today.

Most birds can fly, but an ostrich's wings are too small to lift its large body off the ground. Some bird-like dinosaurs could fly, but the ancient skies were ruled by pterosaurs.

WINGS AND FEATHERS

Dinosaurs developed wings more than 150 million years ago, early on in their evolution. Over time, small theropods such as the Microraptor used their wings and feathers to fly, much like birds today. Modern birds use their strong chest muscles and outer section of their wings, called pinions, to take off and stay in the air.

Most bird-like dinosaurs had teeth, but today's birds do not. This could be because they evolved to have beaks and eat a different diet with nuts and seeds.

Whether a dinosaur could fly or not, feathers were an incredibly helpful covering used for keeping warm and possibly as an elaborate display to attract mates.

Some flying dinosaurs used their tails for balance when walking, and they may have been different colors or patterns. Birds today also have tails, but usually not as long.

Theropods had three toes with long, sharp claws, perfect for attacking their prey. Some of today's birds, including ostriches, have similar feet.

INDEX